BITCOIN: A DUMMIE'S GUIDE TO VIRTUAL CURRENCY

A Simple Guide to Bitcoin Currency, Bitcoins for Sale and Bitcoin Price and Value

By: David Gray

David Gray

TABLE OF CONTENTS

Publishers Notes 3
Dedication 4
Introduction 5
1. What Are Bitcoins? 7
2. Should I Own Bitcoins? 11
3. What about mining bitcoins? 17
4. How to buy and sell bitcoins 19
5. What is the Value of Bitcoins? 24
6 What are the risks involved with owning bitcoins? 26
7. How to Create a Paper Bitcoin Wallet 28
8. Summary: How to buy bitcoins 30
AUTHOR 32

Publishers Notes

BITCOIN: A DUMMIE'S GUIDE TO VIRTUAL CURRENCY: A Simple Guide to Bitcoin Currency, Bitcoins for Sale and Bitcoin Price and Value, Copyright © 2013 by Mix Books, LLC

Print ISBN-978-1508591252

This publication is intended to provide helpful and informative material. No action should be taken solely on the contents of this book.

The author and publisher specifically disclaim all responsibility for any liability, loss or risk, personal or otherwise, which is incurred as a consequence, directly or indirectly, from the use or application of any contents of this book.

Any and all product names referenced to within this book are the trademarks of their respective owners. None of these owners have sponsored, authorized, endorsed, or approved this book.

Always read all information provided by the manufacturers' product labels before using their products. The author and publisher are not responsible for claims made by manufacturers.

All rights reserved. No part of this publication may be reproduced, stored in a retrieval system, or transmitted in any form or by any means, electronic, mechanical, recording or otherwise, without the prior written permission of the author.

mix-booksonline.com

David Gray

Dedication

For the risk-takers and deal-makers. May you be wealthy *and* wise.

Introduction

Bitcoin is a virtual (digital) currency made for Internet transactions. If you own Bitcoin, there is no paper or actual coin, what you own is the private cryptographic key that unlocks a specific address. The private key looks like a long string of numbers and letters Unlike national currencies bound by a country's central bank and financial system, bitcoin buyers and sellers transact on a direct (peer-to-peer) basis. Because no central bank controls the amount of bitcoins in the market, and because no country's money or politics have directly affected bitcoin (though that is changing), it is a currency without borders. It can be used anywhere on earth.

Many people want to understand more about bitcoins. Most of the information available is confusing and complicated, though using bitcoins is relatively easy. Once purchased or mined, bitcoins are easy to spend. Here are answers to a few commonly asked questions.

David Gray

1. What Are Bitcoins?

Bitcoin was introduced to the world as the first "decentralized digital currency." Simply put, no central bank or clearinghouse is involved in processing transactions between bitcoin users. That fact is often positively perceived for users concerned about their home country's currency values!

When compared to other alternatives, bitcoins have some advantages:

1. "Peer-to-peer" transactions
2. Lower fees
3. Usable anywhere
4. No pre-established, arbitrary, or pre-required limits
5. Account cannot be frozen

How are bitcoins minted, or who creates them?

Bitcoins are actually generated all across the Internet, by anyone, using a free app known as a bitcoin miner. Mining requires some work for each block of coins, and this amount is network-adjusted so that bitcoins are always created at a "predictable rate."

Bitcoin's leadership determined that no more than 21 million bitcoins will ever exist. About half of the so-called bitcoin treasury are currently mined and in use. Most users believe that a known quantity of bitcoins over a specific period of time (by the year 2140) should help bitcoins' value increase over time.

Users familiar with Internet banking will quickly understand how to use the bitcoin wallet. To transfer bitcoins to another user requires an electronic signature. After several minutes, the bitcoin transfer is verified by a miner, then permanently and anonymously stored in the network.

Do bitcoins trade on the foreign exchange market?

Every currency on the planet floats against the value of other currencies on the foreign exchange market. The foreign exchange market is the largest trading forum in the world. Governments, corporations, and individuals acquire currencies or hedge against foreign exchange movements on the forex market. Very large amounts of currency using borrowed money (called leverage) allow traders to make or lose money on short-term price movements.

Most people in the United States do not know that the value of the U.S. dollar changes against other currencies on a constant basis. They use dollars in a physical wallet or on the Internet. They do not worry about whether or not their dollars will be accepted for purchases.

Yes, forex trading--even in stable currencies like the U.S. dollar--can be very risky! That is why no one should be surprised to learn that a new currency like the bitcoin is considered an uncertainty.

Can I exchange bitcoins for another currency?

Some currency exchanges enable bitcoin users to exchange their currency to dollars, euros, pounds, etc.

Unlike U.S. dollars, bitcoin is not backed by the "full faith and credit" of any sovereign nation. Theoretically, bitcoins do not rely upon "trust," according to Satoshi Nakamoto (a believed pseudonym for bitcoin's creator). Because bitcoin users trade "peer-to-peer," without any central bank's involvement, it is possible for holders to buy or sell goods and services without the concerns of politics, interest rates, or printing press inflation.

Are bitcoins volatile?

Bitcoin is a highly volatile currency. It is a new currency and, although many other virtual currencies have followed bitcoin's lead, it represents a new financial idea.

China's central bank recently banned financial institutions from dealing in Bitcoin, though individuals are still free to transact. Meanwhile, the world's largest exchange for Bitcoin, BTCChina, recently decreed that it would stop accepting deposits in renminbi – the official currency of the People's Republic of China. In other words, the Chinese can't buy Bitcoin. Also, the U. S. Treasury has recently given notice that, if you are a business accepting Bitcoin, then it is watching you. All of which has added to the currency's volatility. Of course, as discussed above, bitcoin *is* risky. However, for too many reasons to discuss here, even some nations in the Western world have experienced financial crises. In fact, the global economic recession that began in 2008 pointed out how quickly financial woes spread from one country to another.

Earlier in 2013 traders around the world snapped up bitcoin for many reasons, including rapid price appreciation. For example, bitcoin traded in the mid-$200 range in September 2013. Prices climbed as high as $1,240 in the first week of December!

This meteoric and euphoric rise in the price of bitcoin made the subsequent sell-off almost inevitable. According to the Mt. Gox bitcoin exchange, bitcoin traded as low as $576 with a weekly average price of $722. By the end of 2013, the price was generally below $600.

David Gray

2. Should I Own Bitcoins?

Most investors of any highly volatile security or currency understand the importance of risk and reward. For example, a highly volatile or thinly traded currency, rises or falls much more quickly than other widely available and actively traded currencies.

Buying and holding bitcoin may make sense for anyone interested in acquiring it for the long-term. Viewed from a longer-term perspective, a buyer of bitcoins uses any sell-off from speculators to buy more bitcoins at a lower price.

Think about it this way: a buyer of a high quality stock decides that a long-term investment makes sense. She buys some shares today, with the idea that she will buy more if the stock price declines. This is called "cost averaging" and helps the buyer own more shares of the corporation over time at a lower cost basis. When she decides to sell shares at a favorably high price, she will make a higher return on investment.

Because bitcoins are not a national currency, owners naturally bear more risk. However, an original bitcoin--worth about $25 in 2008--was recently worth more than seven figures!

That is the reason so many people are buying and selling bitcoins, and that is why it is important to learn the fundamentals of buying and using bitcoin.

I am interested in buying bitcoins for their long-term appreciation potential. Is there any way to avoid a deep sell-off?

Let's say you decided to sell bitcoins on a ten percent market decline. Unfortunately, because the market is thinly traded, you might "lose the market" before your sell order is executed on a bitcoin exchange.

Some people use over-the-counter derivatives (http://psychologicalinvestor.com/lib/real-markets/bitcoin-derivatives-liquidity-counterparty-risk-134/), when they can find a counterparty. Most major options dealers will not act as a counterparty in a bitcoin derivative transaction.

But, in the event a counterparty is found, you could consider buying bitcoins and then buying and/or selling over-the-counter puts and calls. An OTC option gives the buyer or seller the right to buy or sell a bitcoin for a certain price over a specific term.

It is especially difficult to structure an OTC put or call during a bitcoin sell-off. If you are a long-term holder, consider exploring how to structure puts and/or calls on bitcoins in a stablized market.

I am an Internet seller and some people have asked if I accept bitcoins. Is this a good idea?

Many business owners and freelancers say "Yes!" Because it is easy to start accepting bitcoins as payment, and because processing fees
 are quite a lot less than competitors like PayPal, accepting bitcoins can make sense.

However, not all businesses accept bitcoins as payment. Before making a decision to enter the bitcoin economy, learn whether or not your product or service fits well into it.

What kinds of things can I buy with bitcoins?

David Gray

Videogames, mobile apps, servers, and services related to digital communications can be bought with bitcoins. Freelancers performing services to the digital communicators or e-tail vendors can receive bitcoin payments.

Gifts, books, hand-crafted items, and lots of other things can be purchased with bitcoins.

Bitcoin Travel or Bitcoin Navigator can help identify restaurants, shops and other venues that accept bitcoins.

The list is growing!

Where can I buy and sell with bitcoins?

One of the most popular online sites is Reddit Bitmarket (http://www.reddit.com/r/bitmarket).

-->People have bought or sold large items, include cars and houses, using bitcoins.

Other popular bitcoin sites include:

- Gyft, (http://www.gyft.com/) a specialized mobile app interface, allows users to spend bitcoins for merchandise--
- even when the stores do not directly accept the virtual currency!

- Bitspend (http://www.reddit.com/r/BitSpend/) similarly helps shoppers use bitcoins on popular sites, such as Amazon.com.

Bitcoin: A Dummie's Guide To Virtual Currency

- Bloggers can pay for WordPress.com services with bitcoins. And people with an interest in online dating can pay OkCupid from a bitcoin wallet.
- The BitCoinStore.com is a very popular site offering a wide range of electronics tools at great bitcoin prices.
- NameCheap.com accepts bitcoins in payment for domain registration and hosting services.
- Private Internet Access allows privacy-seeking Internet users to pay for VPN services with bitcoins.
- Some precious metals dealers, such as Coinabul (http://www.coinabul.com) or Amagi Metals (http://www.amagimetals.com/bitcoin), now accept bitcoin as payment.
- BitPremier.com offers luxury goods, including apartments, fine art, yachts, and other attractively-priced items.
- SealsWithClubs (https://sealswithclubs.eu/) is an online poker site that accepts bitcoins.
- BitPointsforCharity.org helps those with bitcoins to fund a charity, including Amani Kinderdorf, Free Software Foundation, Freedom Box Foundation, Nonprofit Recycling and Exchange Network, Vaizard Institute, and WikiLeaks. Ask your tax advisor about how to claim deductions made with bitcoins.
- SpendBitcoins.com helps bitcoin users convert currency to gift cards at Barnes & Noble, Amazon.com, or Apple/iTunes.
- CoinDL is a marketplace for e-books, downloadable materials and content, music, wallpaper, etc.

How do I find local bitcoin users and the bitcoin economy everyone is talking about?

David Gray

A local meet-up group is a good source of information about Satoshi Square events. Buyers and sellers come together in an outdoor forum, such as a Union Square New York City meetup in May 2013.

LocalBitcoins (https://localbitcoins.com/) connects traders in 4197 cities, in 192 countries around the world.

Check local Craigslist posts but, of course, take special care to meet any potential buyer or seller in a public place. In-person theft does happen, according to a Reddit post. (http://www.reddit.com/r/Bitcoin/comments/1b89wm/)

Do I need to understand the technology and open-source code to use bitcoins?

Bitcoin software is completely open source and accessible to anyone for free. Knowledge is power! Even greater ideas happen when everyone with a desire to understand bitcoin's code digs in. If interested, check it out at http://bitcoin.org/en/

But, for most people, the answer is "Probably not."

Depending on the investment made in bitcoins, including the decision to accept and receive significant payments, understanding algorithms, e-signatures, anonymity, and security processes are probably unnecessary or impossible.

Anyone who has ever opened a virtual financial trading account understands that hackers sometimes succeed in collecting personal financial information from the Internet. And, even if the bitcoin network is the most secure in the world--and many proclaim it is-- any network can be hacked.

Yet most people today choose online accounts because, most of the time, these tools make life easier. We get paid, or pay others, for goods and services faster, and receive what we want with greater ease.

David Gray

3. What about mining bitcoins?

Glad you asked! Bitcoin mining is a hobby for some and a passion for others. Because it is a complicated task, many Bitcoin users decide to work together to mine Bitcoins. This shares both time and effort involved.

Because Bitcoin is a decentralized currency (explained above), no central bank or financial authority controls the bitcoin money supply. The work of managing the number of bitcoins is spread throughout the network of users. Most of the labor-intensive work involved in mining is done by "miners."

Miners collect, then bundle, all bitcoin transactions from the network. For example, Sally sends Ari 20 bitcoins" and "Serge sends Galina 5.1 bitcoins." These bundles of transactions are known as bitcoin blocks. Blocks form an unbroken string of transactions known as the "block chain." The chain is evaluated for any conflicts, because no user can apply the same bitcoins more than once! (To do so would be like writing a bad check!) This process counts all transactions and maintains balance.

So far, this sounds pretty easy, but making a block chain is a complicated process. Miners cannot just decide to make a new block, and they must calculate a "cryptographic hash" of the block that conforms to bitcoin criteria. Some miners describe the process as "hashing" and say that a new miner usually tries many until one works. Miners who create a new block receive bitcoins according to a pre-established rewards system. And, in general, increased competition around the world to mine bitcoins has caused most miners to work harder to achieve their goal.

The most successful bitcoin miners buy specialized hardware that works twenty-four hours a day, seven days a week. The hardware

consumes large amounts of electricity, so these costs must be managed by would-be bitcoin miners, too.

Creating a bitcoin chain naturally protects the system against fraud: the work needed to confirm "false" transactions" requires the same amount of work to confirm real bitcom trades.

Bitcoin miners do the difficult work required to "mine" bitcoins that are, as yet, uncirculated. They use special tools to automate and secure the bitcoin network, including:

1. collection of network transactions
2. validation of transactions
3. bundling transactions into blocks
4. identifying cryptographic hashes that meets the "good enough" criteria
5. sending block to the bitcoin network, adds to the block chain, and receiving a reward of bitcoins

If you are interested in learning more about bitcoin mining, start by visiting www.bitcoinx.com.

David Gray

4. How to buy and sell bitcoins

Buyers and sellers, individuals and corporations, can buy and sell bitcoins on an exchange. One of the largest and most respected bitcoin exchanges is Mt. Gox https://www.mtgox.com/signup/activate.

It is easy to arrange an account on Mt. Gox. In less then 30 seconds, new users can activate an account and get a bitcoin wallet. The BTC wallet, like the wallet or billfold used to hold cash, stores bitcoins. There are many bitcoin wallet formats available, and the list is growing very quickly.

The bitcoin wallet is an essential for any bitcoin owner. Exchanges, such as Mt. Gox, offer a wallet as part of the account. Other services, including mobile apps, help buyers and sellers keep track of bitcoins.

Account verification

Mt. Gox requires that each new user verify their identity. This requires an exchange of identification, such as a government-issued driver license or utility account. After verification, the new user may deposit funds into the account to purchase bitcoins. Because Mt.
 Gox new account details say that it can take up to ten days to verify the user's information, buying and selling bitcoins can be delayed.

After the account holder is verified, the new account holder deposits funds, and finally purchases bitcoins.

This delay is a major source of frustration for many people.

For this reason, some hardy individuals buy and sell bitcoins on an open forum, such as eBay.

It is possible to buy or sell one or more bitcoins, or fractions of bitcoins. For example, an eBay seller offers 0.03 BTC at a $29.99 buy-it-now price. He or she requests settlement by PayPal.

Buying or selling small BTC amounts can make sense for both parties. The buyer can average his or her price up or down, and the seller can add a small premium over the current bitcoin price.

How to evaluate a "peer-to-peer" bitcoin sale, such as on eBay

Basic understanding of how eBay works will help a buyer or seller of bitcoins make good decisions:

- Feedback: choose trading partners with good feedback, as close to 100 percent as possible.
- Payment settlement: ask the trading partner to settle the transaction by credit card. Although PayPal senior management appears superficially positive about the long-term prospects of bitcoin currency, PayPal will not protect the user from a bad BTC buy or sell. Use of credit card offers some protection against fraud or bad delivery.
- After completing the eBay purchase, enter your wallet number and select "pay by credit card" from the drop down menu. Alternatively, obtain a phone number from the seller
- and provide your credit card information to complete the sale.
- Make sure to provide your bitcoin wallet information. Without this information, the seller cannot transfer the bitcoins.

David Gray

Other (online) ways to purchase bitcoins

As always, buyer beware! Research any potential trading partner before sending funds to purchase bitcoins.

In addition to Mt. Gox, perhaps the best-known BTC exchange, it is possible to buy bitcoins from other sites, including:

- CampBX.com: wallet, iPhone, iPad, android apps
- Bitcoins.cl: send funds via Moneygram or Western Digital from the U.S.
- rBitco.in--Real BitCoin India: lots of ways to earn money and interest on bitcoin wallet deposits
- 24Change.com: automated bitcoin purchase and sales syste
- BlockChain.info allows users to send bitcoin buy/sell transactions through approved mobile or landline phones (SMS messages) without a credit card, up to three transactions a month
- VirWoX.com: buy bitcoins using credit cards and PayPal
- JustCoin.com Norway: currency exchange, supporting the euro and Norwegian krone, bitcoins, and some virtual competitors
- BitQuick.co: .connects bitcoin buyers and sellers, and enables direct bank transfers. Low transaction fees from bitcoins in escrow.
- CoinMkt.com: cryptocurrency exchange, including bitcoin
- CoinBase.com: buy bitcoins and store in PayPal-like wallet
- BitInstant.com: deposit cash a local mass retailers, such as Walmart or CVS, to purchase bitcoins without a bank account or credit card

OTC trading in bitcoins

Bitcoin: A Dummie's Guide To Virtual Currency

For those with an understanding of how over-the-counter securities of any kind are traded, using the bitcoin otc freenode IRC channel may be an interesting and profitable experience. Here, buyers and sellers may look at open orders. This can help knowledgeable otc traders get a handle on market size.
http://bitcoin-otc.com/

Popular Places to Transact with Other Bitcoin Users
According to the Bitcoin Examiner, the most popular meet-up groups gather in:

1. Israel (http://www.meetup.com/bitcoin-il/) Tel Aviv
2. Japan (http://www.meetup.com/Tokyo-Bitcoin-Meetup-Group/events/110935072/) Tokyo
3. United States (http://www.meetup.com/BitcoinDC/) Washington, D.C.
4. United States (http://www.meetup.com/Miami-International-Bitcoin-Group/photos/) Miami
5. United States (http://www.meetup.com/Silicon-Valley-Bitcoin-Users/) Silicon Valley, CA
6. United States (http://www.meetup.com/San-Francisco-Bitcoin-Social/) San Francisco
7. United States (http://www.meetup.com/bitcoinNYC/) New York
8. United Kingdom (http://www.meetup.com/London-bitcoin-meetup/) London
9. Canada (http://www.meetup.com/Bitcoin-Toronto/) Toronto
10. Switzerland (http://www.meetup.com/Bitcoin-Meetup-Switzerland/) Zurich/Geneva
11. India (http://indiabitcoin.com/meetup/) Bangalore/Ahmedabad
12. Argentina (http://www.meetup.com/Bitcoin-Argentina/) Buenos Aires

David Gray

13. Hungary (http://www.meetup.com/BitcoinBudapest/)
    Budapest

Start a local meetup group in your area to bring bitcoin buyers and sellers together.

5. What is the Value of Bitcoins?

Most people with good common sense answer that the value of a bitcoin is whatever another person is willing to pay for it. But on December 5, 2013, Bank of America's foreign exchange department said that USD1,300 per bitcoin was a fair (projected) value and that a total capitalization of USD 15 billion was also fair.

Bitcoin's coverage by Bank of America both enhanced and supported the virtual currency's prospects, though many other U.S. banks declined to second BofA's enthusiastic assessment.

Since bitcoin is a new currency, it is difficult to determine its ultimate value. As a subjective sense of bitcoin's worth, its value differs from user to user. An individual living in a country with known national currency risk may own bitcoins as part of a financial safety strategy. Another user, intent on buying or selling a service within a community of other robust bitcoin users, wants to attract others in a microeconomy. Still others, of course, want to use bitcoins as a way to avoid watchful government eyes upon their transactions.

Spectacular price appreciation

It is difficult to assess the subjective value of security or comfort that some users find by owning bitcoins.

Market evaluation is easier to determine. According to some bitcoin watchers, 10,000 bitcoins in 2010 are worth $10,000,000 today!

David Gray

On November 19, 2013, Rob Wile of the BusinessInsider.com wrote that 10,000 bitcoins mined in 2010 were worth a mere $6,000,000.

Then, the markets traded higher and lower.

Are Bitcoins for Me?

It is impossible to predict the future of any currency, security, or commodity. Modern Portfolio Theory (MPT) recommends diversification of any financial portfolio for best results.

David Gray

6 What are the risks involved with owning bitcoins?

1. Bitcoin is a new currency without a substantial track record. Publicly or privately issued securities of many corporations rise and fall. Previously successful companies, such as MCI Communiciations, rise, fall, and flouder. **Bitcoins could eventually become completely worthless.**

2. Bitcoin is a freethinking, libertarian kind of currency. It is a brave financial idea that inspires individuals to think beyond the borders of their homelands. However, some governments do not value freedom or freethinking. **Governments could seek to intervene when individuals or use bitcoins, or seek to convert bitcoins into another currency.**

3. Bitcoin users quietly discuss opportunities to earn an income within the bitcoin economy. Many believe that bitcoin earnings are undetectable and untraceable. **As bitcoin capital continues to**

expand in its three primary markets--the U.S., E.U., and United Kingdom--government interest continues to grow.

4. Bitcoin users are reasonably concerned about hackers. **It is possible to lose bitcoins from hackers and malware attacks.** Although no one has successfully hacked the bitcoin network, exchanges and bitcoin repositories have suffered attacks. Recently, hackers made off with about $100 million worth of currency from an illegal drug bazaar. The first known major theft was in 2011 when a user lost half a million dollars. There are also cases of at least one "wallet" service and an investment fund that were scams where investors lost millions of dollars. Lost bitcoins, in this sort of event are, of course, not federally insured!

David Gray

7. How to Create a Paper Bitcoin Wallet

Many online bitcoin wallets, on or off reputable exchanges, exist. Many bitcoin users like Blockchain at the moment. Regardless of the many advantages of an online bitcoin wallet, the threats of loss--from hackers, malware, or even avaricious acquaintances-- makes creating a paper wallet a good idea if you have invested in bitcoins.

Of course, today's paper wallet is not like great-grandfather's cash box or ledger. Instead, the bitcoin paper wallet takes steps necessary to remove keys and transactions' traces from the virtually untold numbers of computers trolling for this information.

Start with Bitaddress.org, or similar, to create the bitcoin paper wallet:

- Use a perfectly pristine operating system. Some bitcoin users recommend buying an older computer with a wiped hard drive for the sole purpose of managing the bitcoin wallet. Ideally, the OS of the computer is not connected to the Internet. -->Open the bitcoin wallet file on a USB drive.
- Create a bitcoin address using the paper wallet service.
- Print the file.
- Then, delete the file, and remove all electronic traces of the shredded file on the computer/USB drive.

Keep in mind that the paper wallet must be kept completely secure at all times. Know yourself: if losing the paper wallet is a possibility, do not risk your bitcoins. Without the corresponding private key to the bitcoin public address, you cannot spend your bitcoins!

Finally, do not make partial withdrawals from the account. Withdraw all bitcoins, then start another paper wallet for maximum security.

David Gray

8. Summary: How to buy bitcoins

1. Bitcoin exchanges:

- Establish a personal or business account with a bitcoin exchange. (Note: business accounts may require more time to arrange.)
- Provide identification as required by the exchange.
- Transfer funds into the account.
- Receive approvable from the exchange that funds are clear. (Depending upon the source of funds, this can take up to 14 days or longer.)
- Inquire about any trading limits. If planning to trade substantial funds, make sure the account is cleared with the exchange to do so. (Don't wait for a brisk trading day to learn you cannot buy or sell!)
- Exchange currency for bitcoins at the current market price.
- Transfer bitcoins to a (non-exchange) bitcoin wallet. Although the exchange provides a wallet, leaving substantial bitcoins there can put bitcoins at risk from hackers.

2. Local bitcoin or other transactions:

- Identify bitcoin users in your area through meet-ups, Satoshi Square groups, etc., who want to trade cash for bitcoins, or who want to liquidate bitcoins for local currency.
- TradeBitCoin.com or LocalBitcoin.com may be helpful in identifying local trading partners.

- Consider eBay.com after researching seller feedback and trade settlement (preferably with a credit card for maximum protection against bad dealers).

3. Bitcoin Payment Services:

- Try a 'fast buy' or 'quick purchase' bitcoin service, e.g. BitInstant.com, QuickBT.com, or btcquick.com.
- When asked, give the payee address and provide how much in bitcoin you wish to pay.
- Check-out instantly using a credible debit or credit card.
- The payee instantly receives bitcoin funds.

David Gray

AUTHOR

David Gray is a Forex trader but when trading platforms began to accept Bitcoins he decided he needed to research this virtual currency. What he found was a lot of confusion, so he decided to put together a book that would explain Bitcoin in a simplified way.

Also by David Gray:

Forex Trading: A Guide To Day Trading Essential Tips

Simple Strategies To Earn Pips Per Day

Printed in Great Britain
by Amazon